Poems For: People who want to be left the f*** alone

Uplifters Press

Esme Redwine

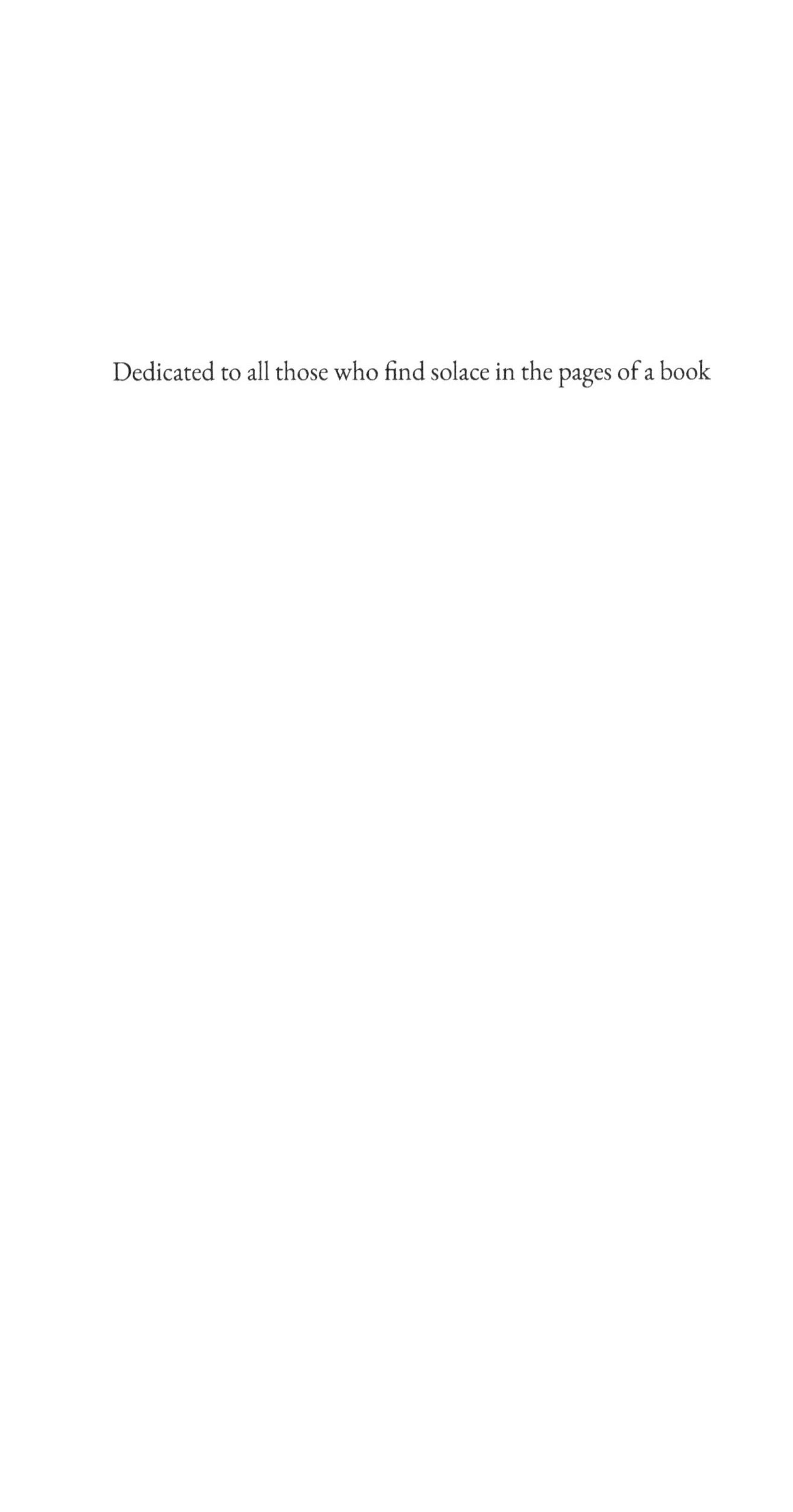

Dedicated to all those who find solace in the pages of a book

Contents

Part I: Hibernation

The World is Too Large Today

In this space it is quiet, where you
breathe in the air around you
and it holds you gently in return.

I am loved in the spaces I put love into.

Early Spring

wind skipping through the tops of trees

as if a returning flock of birds dipping down to skim across the water,

creating soft waves on the surface as they land,

bringing the warmth of late March.

down the road the houses begin the slow process

of exiting their long hibernation, windows open,

gardens just bringing forth soft blooms.

by now the noon sun has quieted,

slowing and thickening the space around it,

softening the light as it pours forth across the rooftops,

spilling a soft-gold into windows,

illuminating the year as it bursts back into life

Waking Up

Silence never absolute, but soft-bellied,
some far-away bird song or alarm
always at the edges of pulling it away.

By the window

To hold the space around you
Close as a blanket.
To let the sun dapple through
The window-shade, caress
Your face, trace a
Love-letter in warmth.
To reach through space to far-away stars,
Hold the whole universe
In the white-paned window.

Late afternoon

When the sun hangs
In perfect silence,
Looking down at the
Horizon, as if to say,
"I am coming
Home to you,
I will warm you
With my light"

Coming home

learn to find love in the soft corners of your body,

to worship the limbs which have carried you all this way,

to forgive the stretches and dimples,

to love the flesh in which your soul finds home

For a moment

either the last strands of moonlight or the new growth of a spiderweb,

tangled around the edges of the coffee maker,

glimmering just for a moment

before the sun emerges and it is swept

away in the routine of morning

Part II: Space to grow

Unbecoming

fingernails,

darkening their half-moon white into the soft umber of earth,

fingers fleshy and soft against the crumbling roots and prickly stems,

letting my body invade the ground slowly, past worms and centipedes, watching

their many legs moving furiously, faster, faster, as if they can outrun

the slow destruction of their world,

and as I reveal the dark recesses of their underground lives,

I wonder how I am any different.

Past Lives

someone sits next to me on the bus,

And for a moment our lives intersect,

whole histories leading to one shared moment

To Loss

I have known you in the empty room down the hall,

where you hovered by the bedside, and when I breathed

you slipped inside me, let the great animal weight of you

spread throughout my limbs. Through you

I have seen this home as an anchor in the dark sea,

forgotten on the seabed, able to withstand the rolling waves of the storm

Giving myself a love letter

To breathe in silence

Is to give the soul

Space to grow

I don't want to go, but I still want to be invited

Life nothing if not contradiction,

Each party a bore of small talk and uncomfortable conversations,

all the while the strange thrill of existing as a recurring character in someone else's life

Old records

The bookshelf pocked by the records you gave me

too-large corners sticking out, flashing the bright album art
and white teeth of old pop stars

On top of the wood the old record player whines out the
music, filling the afternoon

with the slow tempo of old favorites we used to dance to

The notes where I would step on your toes, spin too wide,
settle into a waltz before tripping

to the floor,

falling into the rug – into you – into the easy rhythm of love

All the while the record needle travelling across the dark
mountains and valleys

Of the soundtrack of our lives

As the music plays

the room comes to life with it,

its whole body - lamp, bedpost, window shade - all
thrumming to the same tempo,

the same animal joy

I may be the loneliest person in the world

But that does not stop me from loving all of it,
early mornings punctured by strong cups of coffee,
yellowed pages, dirty boots, thick mud
rolling slowly down the road after a storm. Love
for the days spent adventuring
through the great reaches of the world,
even alone, even cold and tired, even knee-deep in dirt.
Love for the stories I have yet to tell, yet to discover.
Love for the thick river which pushes down to the sea,
which continues running into the face of the unknown,
loses itself in a vast ocean of water. Love for the thousand
beats of wings, for the mayflies which will die tomorrow,
but for today hum boldly,
their many voices carving a space in the air.

Part III: Anthem for a quiet life

I wonder what the world would be through the eyes of my kitchen sink

watching my life pass by in the mountain of dishes,

gathering and melting as the day darkens,

swept away in the harsh run of water.

to mark days in oil stains and soy sauce,

forks dropped down the drain that clang a discordant harmony.

the long wait in darkness,

passing the many hours of the day empty until I come home again.

Birdseye

(floating, maybe flying, above the earth and everything looks different)

It's almost like a quilt,

brown fields stitch into cornflower blue,

Form here you can hear the sunlight stammer, and birds curl down your face like hair,

From here

The world seems to tremble

Listen,

The wind blows so softly

Anthem for a quiet life

Silence not the absence of things to say,

but a creature of endless possibility, all that could be said

Blue

Blame your parents, blame the ground beneath your feet,

blame the vast gravity of planets, blame the coffee pot,

blame the faucet, neither of us able to own up to cracking it,

blame the one leak we cannot stop from dripping,

blame droplets that turn into rainstorms,

blame the determined dog which jumps into the thunder - all wet fur and tail thrashing,

blame muddy paw prints tracked across the rug,

blame tired morning sprawled on the couch together,

trading stray thoughts and insults, blame budget angst

and household blues,

Blame anything but me.

Second dates

Thursday we say goodnight on the porch
Bleached a pale teak color
By standing under many years of sun,
Shuffling awkwardly around
Each other, finding space
For new people in the
Patterns of an old home.

Two types of people

Two types of people
Either the bold or the timid,
As a rule - avoid both

Part IV: Other people

Other People

All slicked-back and smooth-tongued,

Able to smooth over the syllables I stumble on

Bookshelf

As a forest on the rock shelf by the sea,

whose contents bleed out in odd parcels: the rounded
typeface

of gnarled roots blackening the sand, odd oyster shells and
tear-drops,

scraps of ribbon threaded through pages

like the smooth wing of a seabird — rippling soft and blue.

I thumb their many pages and later dream of a few words, —
'ridge', 'glinting', 'carbon' —

set adrift on the oceans of their passions.

Lazy days

Sunday morning after breakfast,

the apple cider donuts on the counter,

the world grows slowly sweeter

The bedroom light my own moon

which I dream to, surround the edges of its light with my hands

as if I hold a glowing planet in my palms, a ghostly fire.

in quiet moments, the universe spills in around me,

the soft glow blooms under my hands.

With you

Each moment sweeter than the one before,

every bad joke or wasted word spinning the seconds into fine gems

At the end of the day

The day grows older, overrun
With missed calls and unfinished errands,
Crumpled love notes,
The whine of faw-away traffic
Pulsing the air – while down
The road a teen spray-paints
The garage an angry yellow,
A neighbor steps outside to water their garden
And laughs at the sight.
Commuters pile up along roads
And train stations on their way
Back from work, all the world caught
In the strange, loud thrum
Of the late afternoon
Rush. Even now the world grows
Weary, even now among the many
Weeds we find ourselves

Returning home

Acknowledgements

This book would not have been possible without the continued support of Uplifters Press, and the lengths they go to to support local voices. I am immensely grateful to be a member of their community writers project. My heartfelt thanks also goes to all those (at Uplifters and beyond) who have read and edited poems with me, and offered advice throughout the publication process.

'Poems For' has always been a series I hoped would be a way to speak to people and let them know that they are not alone, and I appreciate all those that recognize that vision and continue to spread it with tenacity, good humor, and kind hearts.

Lastly, to you, my dearest reader – thank you for making this book a part of your journey. It is you who I am most thankful for.

About the Author

Esme Redwine is the author of 'Poems For', a series of poetry books aimed at speaking to the unique human soul. Esme grew up in Ōtautahi Christchurch and currently resides in Tāmaki Makaurau Auckland, New Zealand. She can often be found with a warm cup of tea and a notebook in hand.

Uplifters Press is an independent publishing house based in Auckland, New Zealand that publishes books focused on uplifting the human spirit. Genres include art and design, self-help, creative writing, nature and cooking.

UP
UPLIFTERS PRESS

www.ingramcontent.com/pod-product-compliance
Lightning Source LLC
LaVergne TN
LVHW052107160826
845678LV00015B/3415